POEMS OF LOVE

DAVID SUGARS

Write and Release
PUBLISHING

5005 Dalhousie Dr NW
Unit 175 Calgary, AB
T3A 5R8, Canada

Contents

Acknowledgement

Special thanks to Write and Release Publishing Company and to Kerri Anne for helping me with my book.

In memory of my wife, Mary. To my children, Jason and Jennifer, thank you for your love and support. I would also like to acknowledge Mark McGregor for his encouragement.

Thank you to those people who supported me. To all the people who want to love, I wrote these poems for you.

Lastly, I dedicate this book to my children, grandchildren and great grandchildren.

Love

Love for some is a hug,
Love for some is a kiss,
Love for some is being together.

and

Love for some is sex.
Love for some is understanding.
Love for some is caring.
Love for some is happiness.
Love for me is this and more,
Love is beautiful
You can't express it!

Love is unique in its way. Love for me is trusting. Love for me is believing. Love for me is respect. Love is honor and faithfulness. Love is beautiful for the love of a woman. She can be so beautiful, eloquent and it's so dramatic.

I love her so passionately and romantically and tenderly because my love is so deep. I gave all my love to one woman. My love will grow substantially more and more until my love is unconditional. The best love that you can give to a woman!!

Without a doubt, love is so unique. A love with no reason! Why? because I want to be loved again.

Love is very unique! Love is different in every person. Love always conquers everything! To me, loving a woman is beautiful and lovely!

Because a woman's love will be faithful! For me, that is Love.

-David Sugars

Have You Ever Pray

Have you ever prayed a prayer
And felt that God just wasn't listening
Or has there been a time
When you felt God turned his back on you.
There has been a time in my life
When I thought God had let me down.
I have prayed so many prayers
For my wife that was dying.

When God took my wife home
I was angry, for I didn't understand why.

I keep asking the Lord, why did you take her?
She was so precious and innocent.
There were many days and nights.
I cried out to God, to justify this to me.
Then, one day God spoke to me.
He said "who are you to read the future?"
Only I know the future for your wife.
It was so much more merciful
For me to take her now.
Than for her to live out the pain,
That I foreseen in her future.
The Lord does answer prayers.
Things don't always turn out the way we want them to be.
But we have to trust in God.
And I know that he knows what is best.

Dedicated to Mary...

-David Sugars

I Wasn't Alone Anymore

Yesterday I was walking alone,
Looking for something I couldn't find.
Walking in circles around my mind,

Too many roads to walk alone.

Will I ever find myself?
Or will I always be lost and alone
It's like walking in a circle again
And there's no way to get out.
I wanted so much to touch the world
But I was afraid it might hurt,
Tiredness fell on me
I stopped to rest my weary body.
You said you'd walk those roads with me
Now, I have found what I was looking for
Today, I touched the world with you
I wasn't afraid and it didn't hurt me
Today, I found something I can't explain
There's a beautiful free feeling inside of me
Today, I found you to help me along
I wasn't afraid anymore.

I wasn't afraid anymore.
Since I found you.

- David Sugars

The Real Me

Who really am I?
What are my real feelings?
I really don't know the real me!
Or who I really am?
Will I ever find myself?
Or will I be lost forever?
It's like walking in a circle!
And there's no way to get out.!
What is the real me like?
Why can't my real feelings show?
They are hidden away inside of me!!
I keep looking and hoping that it will come out.
Who really am I? Am I something else, or am I a writer or a poet?
Who really am I?

- David Sugars

Christmas

Christmas time is a time to be loved and love one another.
Christmas time is a love between a man and a woman,
Their love can grow so much at Christmas time.
Christmas is magical and beautiful.
Christmas is the time to be close to each other.
A time for remembering all the good things that has happened to us and the love that we have for one another.
It is so beautiful at Christmas time and throughout the year.
Christmas time is magical and anything is possible at Christmas time.
Christmas means a lot to many people.
Looking at the stars, Christmas is magical.
If you wish upon the stars at Christmas time,
it's so magical.
But if you want to be in that story, you can be whoever you want to be.
If you reminisce about our future at Christmas time.
The happiness and thousands of miles away,
Christmas brings it all together.
Christmas is a time to laugh, be happy, and not cry.
But most importantly, Christmas is a time for us to be together as a family.
As for you my love, I will love you forever!

- David Sugars

Putting the Past Away

Putting the past away, and start to love one another.
Honey, the way we desperately need to love one another.
I'm not ashamed to say I need you honey or to love you.
I'm not ashamed to say I understand you and I want you desperately.
I may have fooled myself thinking I could be happy without you.
Everywhere I go no matter what I do, you are in my thoughts, in my mind every moment.
In everything I say or do, you are there in my mind.
I can't live without you, honey.
We should love in our hearts one another as we feel things for each other.
And as our love grows, we take the chance to understand one another.
We should respect, honor, cherish, trust and have faith for each other.
For I know that the love I have for a woman is beautiful.

The jukebox plays the love songs of yesterday.
How I wish I could write and feel of my heart in a song for you.
Love songs make me want to cry, because I feel so much of what they say.
I wish somehow I could express the way my heart feels toward you honey.
I always wanted to be a poet and a writer but I just could not write the words of a song for you.

I always wanted to play the songs that speaks about the feelings that I have for you. Somehow, you have forgiven me and gave us one more chance.
I know now that my place is with you!
It takes so much for me to learn that but most of all,
I wish that I could be with you forever.
The pain of not being with you breaks my heart.
That is true, and I hope you understand what I was going through!

- David Sugars

A Lonely Young Man

There was a young man who had no home.
His parents were killed when he was ten years old.
Since then he has been on his own,
playing a guitar and singing his song.
His hair was long and clothes were dirty.

All he has is the guitar and the clothes on his back.
He had no money, just pennies.
When he tried to get a job people just said "go away".
People never talked to him, they called him a bum

Everyone says stay away from him, they never gave him a chance.
At night, he would sleep on the cold ground.
He never had much to eat except for what he found.

Then, one cold night, he fell asleep on the front steps.
In the morning he was found dead, frozen to death.
That's the story of a lonesome young man,
who never knew what it was to be loved.

- David Sugars

So Much Time Has Passed

We know the time has come for us to part ways.
Time has slipped away from you.
I'll always remember the time we had together
It's the last time I'll see you, the last time I'll feel for you.
So much time has passed, My heart aches for you
Did you even think, do you even know what would happen?
This morning, I'll be going to the clouds, We knew this time would come
The hurt is more than you or I can take
For now, I am with the King of the Heavenly Host.
So much time has passed, My heart aches for you
Do they think of you, Do they even care?
Now, he is the King of my heart, He made me everything I am,
He is my morning and my night, He made me see all of Heaven,
For he is the King of the Heavens.

- David Sugars

Beautiful

Beautiful is you
You smile at me and stroke my
lips with tenderness.
Beautiful is you
running free as the wind.

You're running with me,
You hold me in your arms.

The beautification is you as
we play the game of love!
you loving me and I loving you.

- David Sugars

One Day

I learned to listen on that day,
I heard the sounds of laughter and of happy people
But most of all I heard the sound of Love.
Now, I try to listen more often.
Because I know if I listen,
I will hear the sounds of Love again.

— David Sugars

King of the Heavenly Host

Now, He is the King of my heart.
He made me everything I am.
He is my morning and my night.
He made me see all of heaven.
For He is the King of the heavens.
Look upon the mountain,
Can you see the beautiful sight,
The King clothes in white satin
In all of His glory.
There's a glow of sunlight in his face
As to shine upon me as to give me life.
Before He came along I was alone in the darkness.
But now he fills me with his glory.

— David Sugars

Time

Sitting in my room looking out the window.
Seeing things to bring back the memories of yesterday.
Remembering all the fun I used to have.
Thinking of the time that has passed, and I can never bring it back.
I sit and think how much my life has changed in the last year.
The things that I used to do are now just memories.
Years have very quickly passed and everything in my life has changed.

I am growing up now, and going into a different world.
Winter snow is melting and the sun is shining brightly.
As I look out my window, I think back on the things of yesterday.
There sits the bike, I used to ride for hours on end.
And there are the secret places I would go to be alone.
The memories are still there, and sometimes I wish I could go back.

Back when I thought time would never pass.
Well, it is over now.
I wish it had not gone so fast.
Slow down and remember the past when you were a kid.
Time flies so fast.

- David Sugars

The Searcher

I search for my soul
But my Soul, I could Not find.
I look for my God.
I look for you, you eluded me.
I Look for you,
And Then, I Found all three
Love speaks its own language.
I may not tell you about the love in my heart.
All my dreams, happiness and plans, you are a part of them.
But Still I'm sure you understand
At least to some Degree
Thank you darling for the most
Beautiful Present of my Lifetime.

Your Love,

-David Sugars

Segregation

Do we have the right to segregate people?
Do we have the right to segregate our own people?
Do we have the right to be mean to them?
Do we have the right to feel for them?
Do we have the right to do this to them?
What is our right to do this?
Do we have the right not to look at them?
Do we have the right to deny them their rights?
No man nor the day or the hour have the right.

Do we have the right to segregate people?

Do we have the right? Do we have the right to Segregate our own people? Do we have the right to be cruel to them? Do we have the right to be mean to them? Do we have the right to feel for them? Do we have the right NOW? Do we have the right? Do we have the right to segregate people? Do we have the right?

Do we have the right to segregate our own people? Do we have the right? Do we have the right to do this to them? Do we have the right to not to look at them? Do we have the right to deny them their rights? Do we have the right now? Do we have the right?
Do we have the right to be cruel to them? Do we have the right to be mean to them? Do we have the right to feel for them? Do we have the right now? Do we have the right now? Do we have the right? Do we have the right?

- David Sugars

14

Going Our Separate Ways

We knew that the time would come.
For us to go our Separate ways.

Time slips away from us.
I'll always remember the time we had together
It's the last time I'll have you by my side.
The last time I felt your body close to mine.
In the morning, I'll be getting on that plane.
And you'll be going back to her.
We knew we'd have to go back.

Our love will never last only a short time.
These moments we shared will always be with me.
Maybe our love was wrong, but it was so beautiful.

- David Sugars

Where Have All The People Gone

So much time has passed.
Since I've seen you last
The time seems so long
My heart aches for you to come
Just to see your face or just to hear your voice.
People said they once needed you, where are they now?

But they are not here now.

Do they think of you?
Do they even care?
The hurt is more than you or I can take.
The world was so happy when they served you.
There was so much love in people then.
People said they once needed you, where are they now?

But they are not here now?

Do they think of you?
Do they even care?
If he came now,
Would you be ready to go in the clouds?
Could you say I'm in his fold and I'm going home?
People said they once needed you, where are they now
but they are not here now?
Do they think of you?
Do they even care?

- David Sugars

Spring Thunder

Listen to the wind as the storm approaches.
We hear the thunder in the background, you hear it but you don't see it.
Winter gives away as the ground thaws out.
As a springtime storm approaches,
the flowers had popped up to the ground and
up in the sunlight brings out the flowers.
For what a beautiful sight that is for the springtime,
showers bring everything green.
The miracle of it, all the beauty of the flowers and the green grass.
Springtime is the time for everything beautiful.
Springtime brings out the love of everyone after a long hard winter.
Love is in the air for love is everything to everyone.
The Spring thunder rumbles as we stand,
looking in the doorway and holding each other tightly.
We grab one another's arms firmly and hold each other and love each other
for thunder is another form of love.

The thunder rises in our hearts for one another.
Our hearts are like springtime, we love one another.
Love of a man and a woman is so beautiful and so precious and so romantic
and passionate.

With springtime thunder it brings up everything wonderful.
Everyone we know will approach summer and our love will flourish for
each other.
When love for each other flourishes, our love will grow.
We love one another.
Because our love is forever.
Love is like the springtime thunder each year.
Our love will last forever.

- David Sugars

Time is Over

This time, we know it is over.
The love we once shared
Has slowly slipped away
Now, we have to go
Our separate ways.
The promise we made
Are all broken
The dreams we shared
Have all drifted away
We thought love
was forever.
But now you're walking
out that door.

- David Sugars

Are You Ready

Are you ready?
Are your sins forgiven?
No Man knows the day or hour.
None but the Father in heaven
If he comes this minute
Would you be ready?
Could you say I'm in Christ?
Would he receive you?
The time is near.
Be ready to be with the Father,
Pray for forgiveness of thy sin,
Do not wait too long to make things right,

Because it might be too late.

- David Sugars

Happiness

What is happiness?
What really makes you happy?
Can you find it in everything?
Happiness is being happy, really happy
You have a good feeling inside of you
Happiness is having Joy.
Where do you find happiness
Sometimes, you can find it in people
Sometimes, you can find it in what you do
But most of all, you have to find happiness
Within yourself.

- David Sugars

Expressing

How do I express myself?
How do I show that I care?
What are the words to express my feelings?
I know they are hiding somewhere.
There are so many questions in my mind.
But there are no answers for them.
Will I ever know the answers?
Or will they remain unanswered.
I want to show that I love you.
But what are the words to fulfill it?
I speak words but they don't make sense
I touch but there is no feeling.
How do I express myself?

- David Sugars

The Queen of Love

She was a Lady of Heart.
She was a lady of Knowledge.
She was a Lady of Beauty.
She was the Queen of love.
Queen of love, Oh how I love her, Queen of Love.
She knows no danger.
She knows all things.
She knows all love.
The Queen of love, A Queen, A Queen of Beauty.
Oh! how I love her Beauty.
She was lovely.
She was sexy.
She was exquisite, in all her Beauty,
She was the Queen of love of All Times,

- David Sugars

You

Yesterday I was walking alone
Looking for something I couldn't find
Walking in circles around in mind,

Too many roads to walk alone
I wanted to touch the world
But I was afraid it might hurt.

Tiredness fell upon me
I stop to rest my weary body.
Today I found something I can't explain.
There is a beautiful free feeling inside of me.
Today I found you to help me along.
I wasn't alone anymore.
You said you wanted to walk those roads with me.
I have found what I was looking for.
Today I touched the world with you
I wasn't afraid and it didn't hurt.

Today, I found you to walk these roads with me! You once said you needed
me! Now you walk these roads with me! I'm not afraid anymore! But I
walked these roads with you now! It didn't hurt now! For I have found
you! And our love for each other!
I dedicated this to the one I love!

- David Sugars

Lady of White Satin

Look upon that mountain,
Can you see the beautiful sight

A lady in white satin.
She's a lady filled with purity.
There's a glow of sunlight in her body

It shines on me and gives me life.
Before she came along, I was alone in the dark
But now she filled me with her desire.
She is the queen of my heart,
She made me everything I am
She is my morning and my night
She made me see the light.
Oh how I love her!
She's the lady in white satin.

- David Sugars

Lady of Love

She is the lady of love.
Every move is happiness

She is like a petal of a flower on a sunny day.
Love is what she speaks in a fresh and loving way.

She was innocent when she walked on this land.
Lady of Love, Lady of Love, Lady of Love,
I Love you.
Lady of Love, Lady of Love, Lady of Love,
I Love you.
Lady of Love, Lady of Love, Lady of Love,
I Love you.
Lady of Love, Lady of Love, Lady of Love,
I Love you.

The sea is her brother and perhaps knows the land.
Maybe, this land is her mother.

She is a Lady of Love, Lady of Love, Lady of Love.
I Love you.

- David Sugars

Love Song of Yesterday

The jukebox plays the long songs of yesterday.
How I wish I could write.
The feeling of my heart in a song for you.
Love song makes me want to cry.
Cause I feel so much of what they say
I always wanted to be a Poet.

But I just can't write these words.
I wish I could somehow express.
The way my heart feels toward you.
The lyrics of a song are everything to me.

I always want to play the love songs that express my feelings.
The love songs of yesterday.

- David Sugars

About the Author

Born on March 31, 1957 in Albany, New York. David has been writing poems since he was 15 years old. He enjoys writing poems and songs. He thinks love is beautiful and so he starts writing poems about love. During his doctor's appointments, he goes to the park and watches people walking by him. Noticing those people who are also in love as David has been married to his late wife for more than 47 years. Despite all their hurdles, they remained married for a lifetime. David's wife unfortunately died of liver cancer.